The
FAMILY
ADVENTURE
JOURNAL

The

FAMILY ADVENTURE JOURNAL

Turn Everyday Outings into Memorable Explorations

CHRONICLE BOOKS

SAN FRANCISCO

ISBN 978-1-4521-6977-4

Manufactured in China.

Design by Anne Kenady Smith.
Illustrations by Liam Ashurst.

10 9 8 7 6 5 4

Chronicle Books LLC
680 Second Street
San Francisco, CA 94107

www.chroniclebooks.com

WELCOME TO

The

FAMILY ADVENTURE JOURNAL

These pages contain all you need to turn a simple family outing into a memorable adventure. Here you'll find fun and engaging ways to explore the outdoors through inspiring activities and interactive prompts that provoke curiosity and turn small adventures into opportunities for curiosity and exciting discoveries. Whether you're taking a walk through your local neighborhood, on vacation, or hanging out in the backyard, this keepsake journal will turn every experience into an exploration the whole family can enjoy.

Each entry opens with space to record the explorers' names, the date, and the location of the adventure, followed by an engaging interactive activity, like designing an imaginary tree house, drawing a detailed bird's-eye-view map, or composing an epic adventurer's ballad. Choose one entry if you have limited time, or fill in several if you're out and about for several hours. The activities are designed to be simple enough to appeal to a range of ages, so you can engage at whatever level works for the youngest members of your group. At the end of the journal, you'll find blank pages for memories and lists, plus a section with family-friendly game, craft, and activity ideas, including instructions for pine-cone bowling, bark rubbings, and scavenger hunts.

Whatever your adventure, this handy companion makes it easy to explore the outside world, connect with one another, and create lasting memories. Now onward to new adventures!

MAKE A MAP

Spend ten minutes walking in a giant circle around the area you're exploring. Notice all the natural and man-made objects that make this place unique. Use the space provided to create a map with labels for each object. Explorers use maps to orient themselves and record their discoveries—big and small—so be as detailed as possible! (Bonus points for figuring out which way is north, based on where the sun is in the sky above you.)

CLOUDSPOTTING

Spend a few minutes looking up at the sky. Can you spot any familiar shapes in the clouds? Are they moving quickly or floating in place? Draw a few of your favorite cloud shapes here.

SMALLEST TO TALLEST

Spend ten minutes exploring the landscape around you, looking for tiny
things and giant things. Make sure to look up, down, and all around. Once
you've gotten a good sense of the place, draw the smallest thing you see
and the tallest thing you see!

DATE

LOCATION

WRITE AN EXPLORER'S BALLAD

Explorers often compose songs about their adventures to celebrate their discoveries and pass the time on long journeys. What song would you compose about your adventure today? Where have you been? What have you seen? Who are the main characters? Write your lyrics here and then sing the ballad as a group.

DATE

LOCATION

WHAT DO YOU HEAR?

Sounds can tell you a lot about weather, animals, and the natural environment. Close your eyes and listen quietly for two minutes. What sounds do you hear? The wind? Trees rustling? Water moving? People talking? A bird chirping? Cars in the distance? List all the sounds you hear.

DATE

LOCATION

PACK AN EXPLORER BAG

Explorers rely on all sorts of tools to help them make new discoveries—tools like magnifying glasses, binoculars, thermometers, and measuring sticks. What tools would you pack in your explorer bag if you were going to spend a few days exploring this area? Draw your bag and tools here.

INVENT A MOTTO AND A FLAG

Spend a few minutes thinking about the things that define the place you're exploring today—the sights, sounds, smells, and landmarks. What qualities stand out to you as the most memorable and unique? Use those things to come up with a motto for this area and a flag to represent what makes this place special.

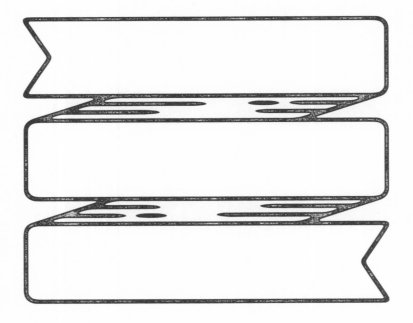

DATE

LOCATION

STUDY A LIVING SPECIMEN

Find something living and observe it closely. What does it look like? How big is it? What color is it? What textures do you notice? How old do you think it is? What does it smell like? Does it make a sound? Use the space provided to record your notes and sketch what you found.

YOUNGEST AND OLDEST

Spend ten minutes exploring the landscape around you, keeping an eye out for things that are young and old. Make sure to look up, down, and all around. What's the youngest thing you can find? Maybe it's a tiny plant or a nest of baby birds. How old do you think your discovery is? Next, look for the oldest thing you can find. Maybe it's a rock, or a tree, or a very, very old structure. How old do you think it is? Use the space provided to record your notes and sketch what you found.

WHAT'S THE WEATHER?

Spend a few minutes exploring the environment around you. What clues
can you discover that tell you about the weather pattern in this area?
Does it seem dry, wet, hot, cold, or windy? Does it seem like a place
where things can grow easily? Take notes on your evidence and observations about the weather.

DATE

LOCATION

TWO TREES

Find two different trees on your adventure today. What do you notice about the similarities and differences in their sizes, bark, leaves, and branches? Do the trees lose their leaves in winter? Do they look young or old? Can you see any clues about how they drop seeds to create new trees? Write your observations, then sketch each tree.

DATE | LOCATION

IMAGINING HISTORY

Close your eyes and imagine what this place looked like throughout history—50 years ago, 100 years ago, and 1,000 years ago. What would be different back then? What may have been the same? Record your thoughts here.

BUILD A NATURE SCULPTURE

Spend 15 minutes looking for natural objects—fallen branches, pinecones, leaves, stones, or flowers, for example. Once you've collected your materials, build a small natural sculpture. Sketch your sculpture here.

DATE

LOCATION

BIRD'S-EYE VIEW

Imagine you're a bird flying high above the landscape. What would you see? Sketch a bird's-eye-view map, adding as much detail as possible (including the members of your group!).

IMAGINING THE FUTURE

Some landscapes change very quickly, while others remain the same for centuries. Close your eyes and imagine what this place will look like in 100 years. What will be different? What will be the same? Record your thoughts or sketch an image of the landscape.

DATE	LOCATION

NATURE BINGO

Can you find all the items listed to win BINGO? Be observant during today's adventure!

SOMETHING GREEN	SOMETHING SMALLER THAN YOUR HAND	SOMETHING THAT GROWS
SOMETHING SMOOTH	MAKE UP YOUR OWN BINGO FIND	SOMETHING ROUGH
SOMETHING MORE THAN 100 YEARS OLD	SOMETHING LESS THAN 1 YEAR OLD	SOMETHING WITH LEGS

DATE | LOCATION

LEAF TRACING

Find a leaf the size of your hand or smaller and trace the outline of its shape here. Then fill in the details.

ADD SOME SIGNS

Signs help explorers orient themselves so they can keep track of their surroundings without getting lost. Imagine you're visiting this place for the first time. What signs would you add to help you keep track of where things are? Create your own signs here. (And remember, signs can include words, pictures, or both!)

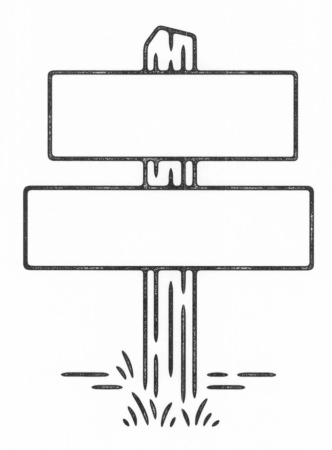

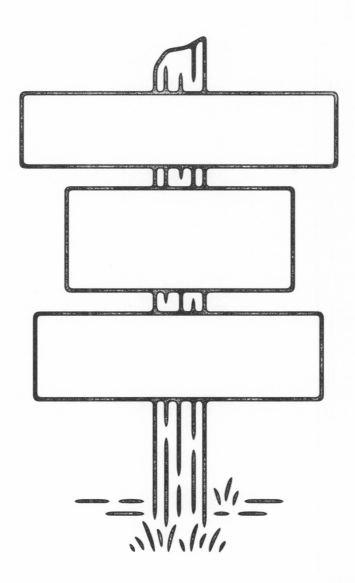

DATE

LOCATION

BUILD A ROCK SCULPTURE

Spend a few minutes collecting stones of all shapes and sizes. Then use the rocks you've collected to build a rock sculpture. You can make a wall or a tower or a spiral or a star. Get creative!

SCAVENGER HUNT

How many of these items can you find? Circle the ones you spot on your adventure.

TREE

ROCK

GRASS

SAND

FLOWER

SIGN

LEAF

BIRD

WATER

BUG

PINE CONE

STUMP

NEST

VINE

DATE

LOCATION

MAKE A MAP

Spend ten minutes walking in a giant circle around the area you're exploring. Notice all the natural and man-made objects that make this place unique. Use the space provided to create a map with labels for each object. Explorers use maps to orient themselves and record their discoveries—big and small—so be as detailed as possible! (Bonus points for figuring out which way is north, based on where the sun is in the sky above you.)

DATE

LOCATION

CLOUDSPOTTING

Spend a few minutes looking up at the sky. Can you spot any familiar shapes in the clouds? Are they moving quickly or floating in place? Draw a few of your favorite cloud shapes here.

SMALLEST TO TALLEST

Spend ten minutes exploring the landscape around you, looking for tiny things and giant things. Make sure to look up, down, and all around. Once you've gotten a good sense of the place, draw the smallest thing you see and the tallest thing you see!

WRITE AN EXPLORER'S BALLAD

Explorers often compose songs about their adventures to celebrate their discoveries and pass the time on long journeys. What song would you compose about your adventure today? Where have you been? What have you seen? Who are the main characters? Write your lyrics here and then sing the ballad as a group.

PACK AN EXPLORER BAG

Explorers rely on all sorts of tools to help them make new discoveries—tools like magnifying glasses, binoculars, thermometers, and measuring sticks. What tools would you pack in your explorer bag if you were going to spend a few days exploring this area? Draw your bag and tools here.

DATE

LOCATION

INVENT A MOTTO AND A FLAG

Spend a few minutes thinking about the things that define the place you're exploring today—the sights, sounds, smells, and landmarks. What qualities stand out to you as the most memorable and unique? Use those things to come up with a motto for this area and a flag to represent what makes this place special.

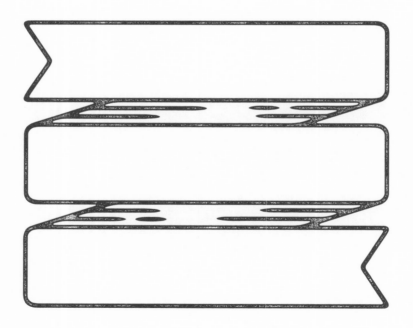

DATE	LOCATION

STUDY A LIVING SPECIMEN

Find something living and observe it closely. What does it look like? How big is it? What color is it? What textures do you notice? How old do you think it is? What does it smell like? Does it make a sound? Use the space provided to record your notes and sketch what you found.

DATE | LOCATION

YOUNGEST AND OLDEST

Spend ten minutes exploring the landscape around you, keeping an eye
out for things that are young and old. Make sure to look up, down, and all
around. What's the youngest thing you can find? Maybe it's a tiny plant
or a nest of baby birds. How old do you think your discovery is? Next,
look for the oldest thing you can find. Maybe it's a rock, or a tree, or a
very, very old structure. How old do you think it is? Record your notes
and sketch what you found.

WHAT'S THE WEATHER?

Spend a few minutes exploring the environment around you. What clues can you discover that tell you about the weather pattern in this area? Does it seem dry, wet, hot, cold, or windy? Does it seem like a place where things can grow easily? Take notes on your evidence and observations about the weather.

DATE | LOCATION

IMAGINING HISTORY

Close your eyes and imagine what this place looked like throughout history—50 years ago, 100 years ago, and 1,000 years ago. What would be different back then? What may have been the same? Record your thoughts here.

DATE | LOCATION

BUILD A NATURE SCULPTURE

Spend 15 minutes looking for natural objects—fallen branches, pinecones, leaves, stones, or flowers, for example. Once you've collected your materials, build a small natural sculpture. Sketch your sculpture here.

DESIGN YOUR OWN TREE HOUSE

Look around and find the best tree for a tree house. What would you want in your tree house? A ladder? Windows? A door? What would the roof look like? Sketch the tree and your dream tree house here.

LOCATION

BIRD'S-EYE VIEW

Imagine you're a bird flying high above the landscape. What would you see? Sketch a bird's-eye-view map, adding as much detail as possible (including the members of your group!).

DATE

LOCATION

NAME YOUR DISCOVERIES

Early explorers named the landmarks, animals, and trees they discovered on their adventures. Imagine you're discovering this area for the first time, and look for interesting objects, animals, or plants to name. Get creative! Then sketch each discovery and label the sketches with the names you've come up with.

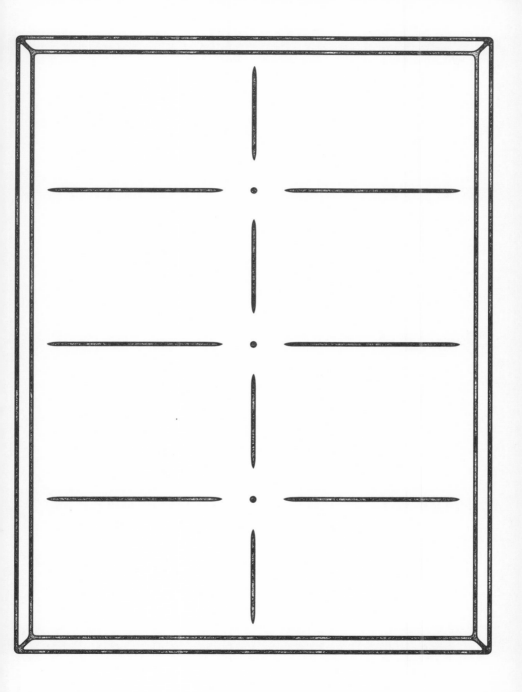

DATE	LOCATION

IMAGINING THE FUTURE

Some landscapes change very quickly, while others remain the same for centuries. Close your eyes and imagine what this place will look like in 100 years. What will be different? What will be the same? Record your thoughts or sketch an image of the landscape.

NATURE BINGO

Can you find all the items listed to win BINGO? Be observant during today's adventure!

SOMETHING GREEN	SOMETHING SMALLER THAN YOUR HAND	SOMETHING THAT GROWS
SOMETHING SMOOTH	MAKE UP YOUR OWN BINGO FIND	SOMETHING ROUGH
SOMETHING MORE THAN 100 YEARS OLD	SOMETHING LESS THAN 1 YEAR OLD	SOMETHING WITH LEGS

DATE | LOCATION

LEAF TRACING

Find a leaf the size of your hand or smaller and trace the outline of its shape here. Then fill in the details.

DESIGN A FORT

Imagine you have to build a fort here for the night. What materials would you use? How big would it be? Sketch your dream fort.

SKETCH A FOOTPRINT

Look for animal prints on your adventure today. Keep your eyes peeled for impressions made by birds, rabbits, deer, squirrels, chipmunks, or even insects. Then use the space provided to sketch the details of your print, with notes on the size of the footprints, how many feet the creature has, and how big you think the creature is. (If you can't find an animal print, you can always sketch your own footprint. Find some soft earth—dirt or wet sand works great—and press your foot into the ground. Then sketch the print)

DATE

LOCATION

ADD SOME SIGNS

Signs help explorers orient themselves so they can keep track of their surroundings without getting lost. Imagine you're visiting this place for the first time. What signs would you add to help you keep track of where things are? Create your own signs here. (And remember, signs can include words, pictures, or both!)

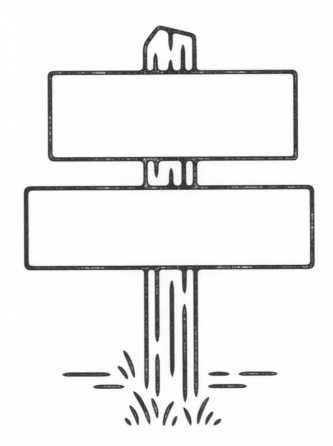

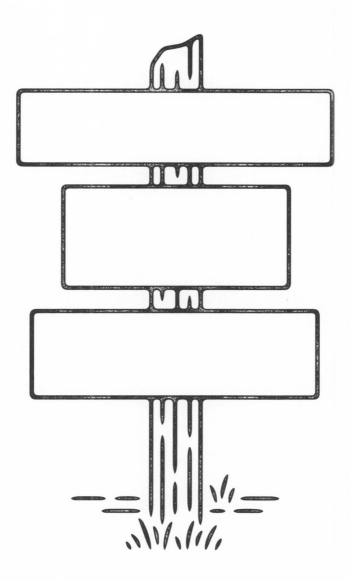

BUILD A ROCK SCULPTURE

Spend a few minutes collecting stones of all shapes and sizes. Then use the rocks you've collected to build a rock sculpture. You can make a wall or a tower or a spiral or a star. Get creative!

DATE

LOCATION

FOLLOW A BUG

It's amazing how much life you can see if you look closely. Get really close to the ground and see if you can find a bug to follow. Then spend five minutes observing the bug's movements. How is it behaving? Is it slow? Fast? Record your notes below!

BUG'S BEHAVIOR:

BUG SKETCH:

DATE | LOCATION

SCAVENGER HUNT

How many of these items can you find? Circle the ones you spot on your adventure.

TREE

ROCK

GRASS

SAND

FLOWER

SIGN

LEAF

BIRD

WATER

BUG

PINE CONE

STUMP

NEST

VINE

DATE

LOCATION

SPOT THE LANDMARKS

Explorers use landmarks to help them figure out where they are and where they're going. What landmarks can you spot in the area you're exploring? Find four objects, then draw and label them here.

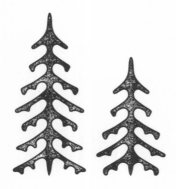

MAKE A MAP

Spend ten minutes walking in a giant circle around the area you're exploring. Notice all the natural and man-made objects that make this place unique. Use the space provided to create a map with labels for each object. Explorers use maps to orient themselves and record their discoveries—big and small—so be as detailed as possible! (Bonus points for figuring out which way is north, based on where the sun is in the sky above you.)

DATE | LOCATION

CLOUDSPOTTING

Spend a few minutes looking up at the sky. Can you spot any familiar shapes in the clouds? Are they moving quickly or floating in place? Draw a few of your favorite cloud shapes here.

DATE | LOCATION

SMALLEST TO TALLEST

Spend ten minutes exploring the landscape around you, looking for tiny things and giant things. Make sure to look up, down, and all around. Once you've gotten a good sense of the place, draw the smallest thing you see and the tallest thing you see!

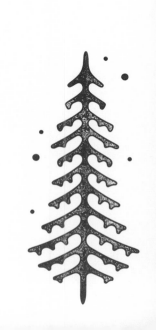

WRITE AN EXPLORER'S BALLAD

Explorers often compose songs about their adventures to celebrate their discoveries and pass the time on long journeys. What song would you compose about your adventure today? Where have you been? What have you seen? Who are the main characters? Write your lyrics here and then sing the ballad as a group.

DATE

LOCATION

WHAT DO YOU HEAR?

Sounds can tell you a lot about weather, animals, and the natural environment. Close your eyes and listen quietly for two minutes. What sounds do you hear? The wind? Trees rustling? Water moving? People talking? A bird chirping? Cars in the distance? List all the sounds you hear.

DATE | LOCATION

PACK AN EXPLORER BAG

Explorers rely on all sorts of tools to help them make new discoveries—tools like magnifying glasses, binoculars, thermometers, and measuring sticks. What tools would you pack in your explorer bag if you were going to spend a few days exploring this area? Draw your bag and tools here.

DATE

LOCATION

INVENT A MOTTO AND A FLAG

Spend a few minutes thinking about the things that define the place you're exploring today—the sights, sounds, smells, and landmarks. What qualities stand out to you as the most memorable and unique? Use those things to come up with a motto for this area and a flag to represent what makes this place special.

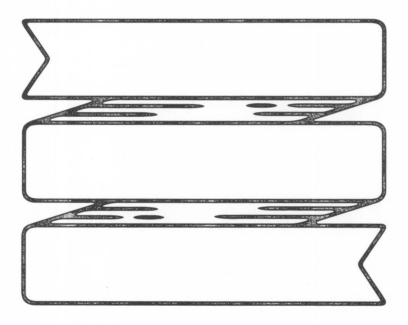

DATE

LOCATION

STUDY A LIVING SPECIMEN

Find something living and observe it closely. What does it look like? How big is it? What color is it? What textures do you notice? How old do you think it is? What does it smell like? Does it make a sound? Use the space provided to record your notes and sketch what you found.

DATE

LOCATION

YOUNGEST AND OLDEST

Spend ten minutes exploring the landscape around you, keeping an eye out for things that are young and old. Make sure to look up, down, and all around. What's the youngest thing you can find? Maybe it's a tiny plant or a nest of baby birds. How old do you think your discovery is? Next, look for the oldest thing you can find. Maybe it's a rock, or a tree, or a very, very old structure. How old do you think it is? Record your notes and sketch what you found.

DATE

LOCATION

WHAT'S THE WEATHER?

Spend a few minutes exploring the environment around you. What clues can you discover that tell you about the weather pattern in this area? Does it seem dry, wet, hot, cold, or windy? Does it seem like a place where things can grow easily? Take notes on your evidence and observations about the weather.

TWO TREES

Find two different trees on your adventure today. What do you notice about the similarities and differences in their sizes, bark, leaves, and branches? Do the trees lose their leaves in winter? Do they look young or old? Can you see any clues about how they drop seeds to create new trees? Write your observations, then sketch each tree.

DATE | LOCATION

IMAGINING HISTORY

Close your eyes and imagine what this place looked like throughout history—50 years ago, 100 years ago, and 1,000 years ago. What would be different back then? What may have been the same? Record your thoughts here.

DATE | LOCATION

BUILD A NATURE SCULPTURE

Spend 15 minutes looking for natural objects—fallen branches, pinecones, leaves, stones, or flowers, for example. Once you've collected your materials, build a small natural sculpture. Sketch your sculpture here.

DESIGN YOUR OWN TREE HOUSE

Look around and find the best tree for a tree house. What would you want in your tree house? A ladder? Windows? A door? What would the roof look like? Sketch the tree and your dream tree house here.

DATE

LOCATION

BIRD'S-EYE VIEW

Imagine you're a bird flying high above the landscape. What would you
see? Sketch a bird's-eye-view map, adding as much detail as possible
(including the members of your group!).

DATE

LOCATION

NAME YOUR DISCOVERIES

Early explorers named the landmarks, animals, and trees they discovered on their adventures. Imagine you're discovering this area for the first time, and look for interesting objects, animals, or plants to name. Get creative! Then sketch each discovery and label the sketches with the names you've come up with.

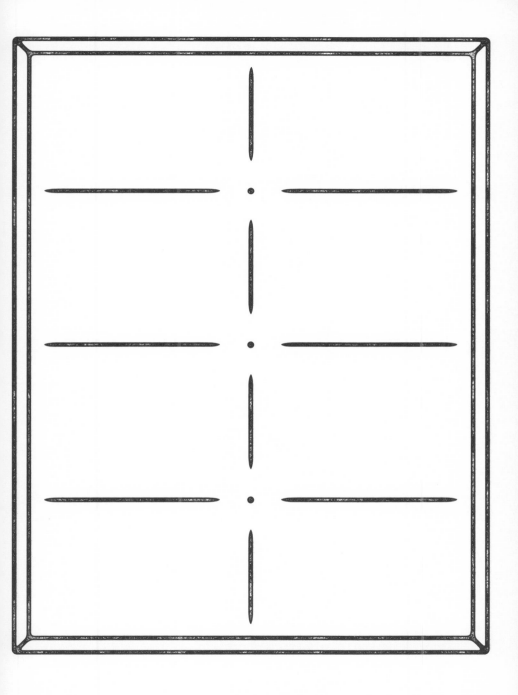

DATE

LOCATION

IMAGINING THE FUTURE

Some landscapes change very quickly, while others remain the same for centuries. Close your eyes and imagine what this place will look like in 100 years. What will be different? What will be the same? Record your thoughts or sketch an image of the landscape.

DATE | LOCATION

NATURE BINGO

Can you find all the items listed to win BINGO? Be observant during today's adventure!

SOMETHING GREEN	SOMETHING SMALLER THAN YOUR HAND	SOMETHING THAT GROWS
SOMETHING SMOOTH	MAKE UP YOUR OWN BINGO FIND	SOMETHING ROUGH
SOMETHING MORE THAN 100 YEARS OLD	SOMETHING LESS THAN 1 YEAR OLD	SOMETHING WITH LEGS

LEAF TRACING

Find a leaf the size of your hand or smaller and trace the outline of its shape here. Then fill in the details.

DATE | LOCATION

DESIGN A FORT

Imagine you have to build a fort here for the night. What materials would you use? How big would it be? Sketch your dream fort.

DATE | LOCATION

SKETCH A FOOTPRINT

Look for animal prints on your adventure today. Keep your eyes peeled for impressions made by birds, rabbits, deer, squirrels, chipmunks, or even insects. Then use the space provided to sketch the details of your print, with notes on the size of the footprints, how many feet the creature has, and how big you think the creature is. (If you can't find an animal print, you can always sketch your own footprint. Find some soft earth—dirt or wet sand works great—and press your foot into the ground. Then sketch the print!)

ADD SOME SIGNS

Signs help explorers orient themselves so they can keep track of their surroundings without getting lost. Imagine you're visiting this place for the first time. What signs would you add to help you keep track of where things are? Create your own signs here. (And remember, signs can include words, pictures, or both!)

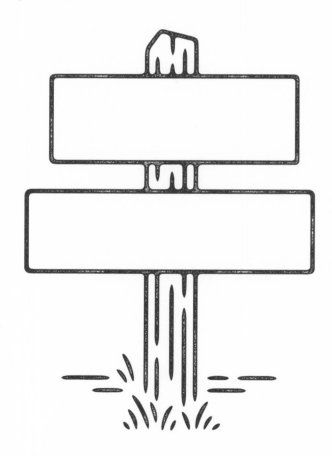

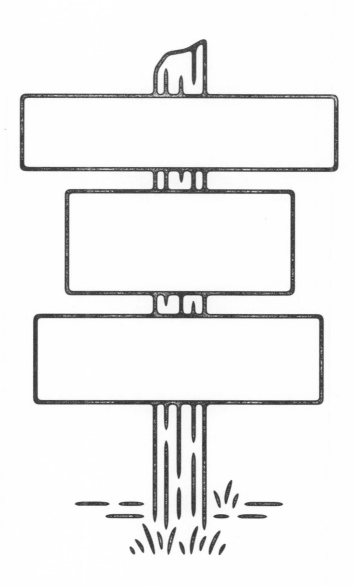

BUILD A ROCK SCULPTURE

Spend a few minutes collecting stones of all shapes and sizes. Then use the rocks you've collected to build a rock sculpture. You can make a wall or a tower or a spiral or a star. Get creative!

DATE | LOCATION

FOLLOW A BUG

It's amazing how much life you can see if you look closely. Get really close to the ground and see if you can find a bug to follow. Then spend five minutes observing the bug's movements. How is it behaving? Is it slow? Fast? Record your notes below!

BUG'S BEHAVIOR:

BUG SKETCH:

SCAVENGER HUNT

How many of these items can you find? Circle the ones you spot on your adventure.

TREE

ROCK

GRASS

SAND

FLOWER

SIGN

LEAF

BIRD

WATER

BUG

PINE CONE

STUMP

NEST

VINE

DATE

LOCATION

SPOT THE LANDMARKS

Explorers use landmarks to help them figure out where they are and where they're going. What landmarks can you spot in the area you're exploring? Find four objects, then draw and label them here.

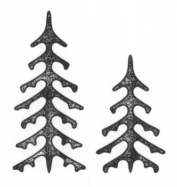

ADVENTURES TO GO ON

ADVENTURES TO GO ON

ADVENTURES WE'VE TAKEN

ADVENTURES WE'VE TAKEN

FUNNY STORIES TO REMEMBER

_____

_____

_____

_____

_____

_____

_____

_____

_____

_____

_____

_____

_____

_____

_____

_____

_____

_____

FUNNY STORIES TO REMEMBER

GAME, CRAFT, AND ACTIVITY IDEAS

TIC-TAC-TOE IN THE DIRT

Materials: Sticks

Directions: Find two sticks—one for each participant. Draw a large board with space for nine boxes in the dirt, then have each participant use the sticks to mark Xs and Os.

BOWLING WITH PINE CONES

Materials: Nine pine cones, rocks

Directions: Find nine pine cones and arrange them in a triangle like bowling pins. Mark a line in the ground a good throwing distance away, then use a round rock or another pine cone as a bowling ball and take turns trying to knock all the pins over. Note: If you can't find pine cones, you can use old water bottles.

HORSESHOES WITH STICKS AND STONES

Materials: Two sticks, rocks (three per participant)

Directions: Place two sticks vertically in the ground a good throwing distance apart. Have each player take a turn standing at the closest stick and throwing their rocks from one end of the course to the other, trying to get a rock as close as possible to the stick at the far end. Whoever gets a rock closest to the far stick wins!

SCAVENGER HUNT

Materials: Paper, writing implement, bags for each participant

Directions: Before you leave home, create a list of objects to find on the scavenger hunt. (Make sure they're things that are already on the ground, like pine cones, pebbles, leaves, and feathers.) Once you get to the adventure site, give each participant a copy of the list and a bag to collect their treasures. Whoever finds everything on the list first wins!

ARCHAEOLOGICAL SITE

Materials: Sticks or string, paper, writing implement

Directions: Mark off a 4-by-4-ft (122-by-122-cm) area using sticks or string. List and draw everything you can find within that area (without disturbing its occupants). Think about the kind of soil it is, and the plants, bugs, and other critters that are there.

NATURE LOGBOOK

Materials: Box or bag, notebook, tape, writing implement

Directions: Bring a bag or a box on your next adventure and collect leaves, seeds, twigs, bark, and other natural materials from the ground. When you get home, tape or glue the materials into a notebook and label each find with the date, location, and a short description.

BARK RUBBINGS

Materials: Paper, crayon

Directions: Bring a few sheets of light-colored paper and a writing implement (crayon works great) on your adventure. Place a piece of paper against a tree, and, using the crayon, gently rub against the tree until the texture of the bark appears on the paper.

LEAF PRINTS

Materials: Leaves, water-based paint, paintbrush, construction paper

Directions: Collect a variety of leaves on your next adventure. When you're home, use a water-based paint and carefully paint each leaf. Then flip the painted side onto a piece of paper and press down carefully to make an imprint.

ADVENTURE PICNIC

Materials: Picnic blanket, plates, utensils, cups, picnic food

Directions: Next time you're at the farmers' market or a grocery store, pick up a few food items that you don't normally eat at home, then pack a picnic for the park or the backyard. Set up your picnic blanket and sample the different dishes, pretending you're on a big adventure where you have to try new and exotic foods for the first time.

ROCK PAINTING

Materials: Rocks, toothpicks, acrylic paint

Directions: Collect a few small rocks on your next adventure. Wash each rock with water to remove any dirt or debris. Let the rocks dry, then dip a toothpick in paint and use the tip of the toothpick to create designs on the rock surface. Let the paint dry, then use the rocks as paperweights, doorstops, or decorations around the house.

COLLECT AND PRESERVE TREASURES

Materials: Found objects and mementos

Directions: Save tickets, maps, or notes from your adventures, and look for other small objects that will lay flat, like grasses, leaves, pressed flowers, and bark (make sure any plant materials are dead—don't harm living plants).